Central England Vol II
Edited by Angela Fairbrace

 Young**Writers**

First published in Great Britain in 2007 by:
Young Writers
Remus House
Coltsfoot Drive
Peterborough
PE2 9JX
Telephone: 01733 890066
Website: www.youngwriters.co.uk

SB ISBN 978-1 84431 216 0

Foreword

Young Writers was established in 1991 and has been passionately devoted to the promotion of reading and writing in children and young adults ever since. The quest continues today. Young Writers remains as committed to the nurturing of poetic and literary talent as ever.

This year's Young Writers competition has proven as vibrant and dynamic as ever and we are delighted to present a showcase of the best poetry from across the UK and in some cases overseas. Each poem has been selected from a wealth of *Little Laureates* entries before ultimately being published in this, our sixteenth primary school poetry series.

Once again, we have been supremely impressed by the overall quality of the entries we have received. The imagination, energy and creativity which has gone into each young writer's entry made choosing the poems a challenging and often difficult but ultimately hugely rewarding task - the general high standard of the work submitted ensured this opportunity to bring their poetry to a larger appreciative audience.

We sincerely hope you are pleased with this final collection and that you will enjoy *Little Laureates Central England Vol II* for many years to come.

Contents

Cranberry Junior School, Alsager

Megan Corlett (9)	38
Annie Tyson (9)	39
Kieran Tucker (9)	40
Anna Weatherburn (9)	41
Rachael Ayre (9)	42
Eden Lily Tagg (9)	43
Chloe King (9)	44
Joshua Arthurs (9)	45
Adam Williams (9)	46

Fieldhead Junior School, Birstall

Nicole Riach	47
Chloe-Louise Parkinson (10)	48
Sophie Manning (10)	49
Amy Leigh Hemingway (10)	50
David Taylor (8)	51
Sara Jane O'Brien (9)	52
Joe Walsh (9)	53
Bradley Parkes (9)	54
Kendell Lucy Doyle (9)	55
Lorraine Sherwood (9)	56
Danielle Taylor (9)	57

Meadows Primary & Nursery School, Ketley

Charlie Price (8)	58
Kelsey Cadwallader (8)	59
Hayley Fergusson (7)	60
Sam Henry (8)	61
Katie Cresswell (8)	62
Samantha Griffiths (8)	63
Lewis Rigby (8)	64
Jake Bradshaw (10)	65
Luke Cadwallader (10)	66
Tammy Woodman (11)	67
Vicky Pope (10)	68
Sophie Banks (10)	69
Sophie-Jane Hodgkinson (10)	70
Liam Norton (10)	71
Charlotte Adams (10)	72
Jashan Bahad (9)	73

St Andrew's CE Primary School, Stanley

St Thomas Aquinas RC Primary School, Stoke-on-Trent

Western Primary School, Harrogate

The Poems

Happiness

Happiness is yellow like the sun in the sky.
It feels like the sea going on the rocks.
It sounds like a bird in a tree.
It looks like kids having fun.
It smells like fresh-cut grass.
It tastes like ice cream.

Joshua Gardner (10)
Borrow Wood Junior School, Spondon

Love

Love is red and pink like one million love hearts in the night sky.
It sounds like enchanted music singing loudly.
It smells like lavender in the summer wind.
It reminds me of family and friends having fun in the sun.
It tastes like a lovely stream of red and white roses.
It feels safe and warm.

Emily Thompson (10)
Borrow Wood Junior School, Spondon

Anger

Anger is red like a massive sun ball,
It feels like some lions' sharp teeth.
It smells like a pig rolling in the smelly mud,
It tastes like a boiling hot curry in your watering mouth.
It reminds me of a mad person running madly,
With a gang with a lot of guns, it frightens me.
It looks like a red knife speared someone's heart.

Brandon Hendy (10)
Borrow Wood Junior School, Spondon

Happiness

Happiness is yellow like stars in the sky.
It sounds like happy tweeting birds in the trees.
It looks like children playing on the streets.
It smells like cooking food in the kitchen.
It tastes like melting ice cream in your mouth.
It feels like sand in your hands.
It reminds me of the day I went to Great Yarmouth.

Josh Bates (10)
Borrow Wood Junior School, Spondon

Happiness

Happiness is yellow like a sweet lemon.
Happiness tastes like the fresh air blowing in my face.
Happiness feels like I'm on top of the world.
Happiness sounds like a soft song on the radio.
Happiness looks like happy children playing in the playground.
Happiness smells like melted chocolate.
Happiness reminds me of my dad helping me.

Angie Woodward (10)
Borrow Wood Junior School, Spondon

Happiness

Happiness is yellow like a flower.
Happiness smells like freshly cut grass.
Happiness feels like feathers rubbing on your hand.
Happiness sounds like a child laughing happily.
Happiness looks like a child playing.
Happiness reminds me of people talking happily.

Jack Biggin (10)
Borrow Wood Junior School, Spondon

Love

Love is pink like sunflowers in a beautiful field.
It tastes like chocolate-shaped hearts of love.
It feels like the best thing in the world.
It reminds me of my mum.
It sounds like echoes of love.
It looks like your mum when you haven't seen her in a while.

Connor Giles (10)
Borrow Wood Junior School, Spondon

Sadness

Sadness is dark blue like the deep sea.
Sadness looks like a dead relative.
It feels like the whole world is against you.
It tastes like raw flesh.
It reminds me of the war.
It smells like a rotten body.
It sounds like a screaming cat.

Joe Turner (10)
Borrow Wood Junior School, Spondon

Fear

Fear is pale white
It feels like I could die
It looks like a girl screaming
It reminds me of people screaming and shouting for help
It tastes like somebody who hasn't had a shower for ages.

Ryan Harris (10)
Borrow Wood Junior School, Spondon

Anger

Anger is red like running blood
It sounds like your heart beating fast
It looks like sick
It smells like trash
It feels like going mad
It tastes like fish food.

Zak Henson (9)
Borrow Wood Junior School, Spondon

Sadness

Sadness is dark blue like the deep blue sea.
It feels like life is just not worth living.
It tastes like snail slime.
It reminds me of my dad when he split up with my mum.
It smells like a bonfire's heart burning.
It sounds like a scream for help.

Michaela Paige Fowle (10)
Borrow Wood Junior School, Spondon

Sadness

Sadness is black like a black heart
It sounds like a tear dropping in a pool of sadness
It reminds me of my grandad when he died, and my dad
It feels like your heart melting like a pound of butter
Guts tearing, limb by limb
It tastes like a ball of tears
It smells like a burning fire.

Michael Payne
Borrow Wood Junior School, Spondon

Anger

Anger is red like a bonfire spitting.
It sounds like an exploding in my head.
It reminds me of chasing my friend with an axe.
It looks like a fireball exploding in front of me.
It tastes like a burning sun in my mouth.
It feels like a piece of burning wood.

Jacob Wroe (9)
Borrow Wood Junior School, Spondon

Fear

Fear is white like a big ball of snow.
It looks like a big wool cushion.
It reminds me of a boiled egg.
It tastes like a really cold ice cube.
It sounds like a bull crying.
It smells like people's stinky breath in my face.

Olivia Gill (9)
Borrow Wood Junior School, Spondon

Fun

Fun is blue as the sea next to the sunny beach.
Fun sounds like children in the sun playing with water guns.
Fun tastes like an ice cream melting in the hot summer days in May.
Fun looks like children splashing themselves with water in the sunny
back garden.
Fun feels like the sun beating over you when you're laughing with
your friends.
Fun reminds me of playing with my friend in the sun or going fishing
in my friend's pond.

Rebecca Flinn (10)
Borrow Wood Junior School, Spondon

Laughter

Laughter is yellow like a sheet of yellow card on a summer's day.
Laughter is as loud as a house dropping from the sky on a
winter's day.
Laughter tastes like a chocolate milkshake on a spring morning.

Ryan Bates (10)
Borrow Wood Junior School, Spondon

Fun

Fun is as bright as the orange sun, burning down on a
midsummer's day.
Fun sounds like the laughter of small children playing in the park in
the middle of August.
Fun tastes like the fresh, fruity flavours of cool drinks on a
summer barbecue.
Fun looks like a bright banner outside someone's house.
Fun feels like the soft sand on my feet when I run along the beach.
Fun reminds me of midsummer birthday parties outside.

Charlotte Wray (9)
Borrow Wood Junior School, Spondon

Laughter

Laughter is as blue as the summer's sky in the afternoon.
Laughter is as loud as an aeroplane crashing into an
enormous mountain.
It tastes like a bar of chocolate melting in your mouth.
Laughter looks as fierce as a black and red fire-breathing dragon.
It feels as coarse as some alligators' bumpy scales.
Laughter reminds me of a long narrow stream falling off a giant cliff
as big as the Grand Canyon!

Harry Mertens (9)
Borrow Wood Junior School, Spondon

Happiness

Happiness is yellow like the glorious sun.
It looks like people laughing and playing in the long grass.
It smells like the watery spicy lemon sizzling in my mouth.

Happiness tastes like the wonderful ice lollies melting in my mouth.
It feels like smooth hot chocolate melting in my mouth.

Happiness sounds like laughing and giggling late at night.

Matt Sharman
Borrow Wood Junior School, Spondon

Darkness

Darkness is as black as the void of space.
Darkness sounds like the wind passing you on a dark night.
Darkness tastes like the air passing through your mouth.
Darkness looks like the blackness of space passing through time.
Darkness feels like a monster mashing up your room.
Darkness reminds me of stars in space.

Daniel Machin (10)
Borrow Wood Junior School, Spondon

Darkness

What colour is it?
Black.
What does it sound like?
Screams in a scary movie and silence, when no one is on the street.
What does it taste like?
Barbecue.
What does it look like?
Time for bed.
What does it feel like?
It feels like when you have just fallen asleep.
What does it remind you of?
Falling asleep.

Jack Underwood (10)
Borrow Wood Junior School, Spondon

Silence

Silence is as black as a dark black chalkboard in a closed school
Silence is as quiet as the sun glowing and shining down on a hot
summer's day.
Silence tastes like a sour lemon on the tip of your tongue.
Silence looks like a bare field on a hot summer's day when no one
is around.
Silence feels like a breeze of coldness running down your back.
Silence reminds me of a blank field on a windy day.

Sophie White (10)
Borrow Wood Junior School, Spondon

Silence

Silence is an array of colours mixing together
like a rainbow glistening in the sunlight of a mid-spring day.
Silence sounds like sitting in a wave of grass.
Silence tastes like nothingness on the tip of my tongue
but with a slice of zangy lime.
Silence looks like someone looking back at their happy memories.
Silence feels like a gentle hand on my shoulder
as I cry for my best friend lying in a grave full of death.
Silence reminds me of sweet runny chocolate.
It also reminds me of my best grandad.

Cerri Minall (10)
Borrow Wood Junior School, Spondon

Hunger

Hunger is as green as a fresh cabbage just been picked.
Hunger sounds like an earthquake starting to rumble.
It smells like black, burnt sausages.
Hunger looks like a buffet of food in your thoughts.
Hunger feels like your belly's going to explode without any food.
Hunger reminds me of food, a big mountain of food.

Aliesha Passey (10)
Borrow Wood Junior School, Spondon

Happiness!

Happiness is yellow as the shiniest sun.
Happiness sounds like people winning the lottery.
Happiness tastes like a chocolate bar touching your tongue.
Happiness looks like a baby bluebird.

Chloe Hicks (10)
Borrow Wood Junior School, Spondon

Laughter

Laughter is the colour of a red apple being eaten.
Laughter is the sound of children playing in the red-hot sun on
a sunny day.
Laughter tastes like a big fat strawberry milkshake with
delicious taste.
Every time I take a sip my taste buds explode like a volcano erupting.
Laughter looks like a little girl playing in the sea with her family on
an empty beach.
Laughter feels like a red-hot boiling sun burning my skin.
Laughter reminds me of when it was my birthday and I invited all my
friends round and had tea and went on the bouncy castle.

Francesca Ruth Roome (10)
Borrow Wood Junior School, Spondon

Fun

Fun is as red and orange as a sour cherry being freshly picked
off a cherry tree on a burning hot summer's day.
Fun sounds like little children screaming with laughter
on the biggest ride at the funfair.
Fun tastes like zingy oranges and zangy lemons
tingling on the end of your tongue.
Fun looks like a blur of colours just like the rainbow
being mixed in a smoothie mixer.
Fun feels like a volcano inside me about to explode
with sizzling lava pouring out.
Fun reminds me of all the fantastic memories
of fun places I've been to!

Miranda Joanne Rea (9)
Borrow Wood Junior School, Spondon

Darkness

Darkness is as misty as rain pouring down in front of your face.
Darkness sounds like death approaching actively towards my heart.
Darkness tastes like the dullness of chocolate.
Darkness looks like danger defending me.
Darkness feels like a cold breeze bouncing off bare arms.
Darkness reminds me of dead people popping out of coffins.
Darkness is death!

Bethany Victoria Mosley (10)
Borrow Wood Junior School, Spondon

Anger Is . . .

Anger is as red as your beautiful rosy cheeks.
Anger sounds like people that are downtown and drunk and
                                    are shouting at each other.
Anger tastes like a big red and very juicy plum.
Anger looks like when you get told off and have to go to
                                        your bedroom.
Anger feels like you're going to blow up.

Connor Webster (9)
Borrow Wood Junior School, Spondon

Silence

Silence is like a clear blue sky on a mild and fresh day.
Silence is like a tree swaying gently and as calm as water flowing
quickly down a shallow stream.
Silence tastes like a breath of autumn and sweet pears that drop
off the brownish trees.
Silence looks like endless fields of wild flowers and calm days when
you're on your own.
Silence feels warm and relaxing and calm.
Silence reminds me of happy times that I spend with my family.

Rebecca Tomlinson (10)
Borrow Wood Junior School, Spondon

Hunger

Hunger is brown as a suntan in the Sahara.
Hunger sounds like 1,000 Victorian miners.
Hunger tastes as bittersweet as butterscotch.
It looks as sickly as the desert becoming longer with every step.
Hunger feels like the white-hot intensity
of a blue super giant star bristling on my face.
Hunger reminds me of the Grand Canyon and Sahara desert's
boiling hot heat of an open oven bristling on my face,
each second creating mirages to send me spiralling
through the corridors of madness as I suffer
from heat, illusions, mirages and madness as I suffer
from boiling heat in the Grand Canyon and Sahara desert
put together against me to send me mad.

Reece Walker (10)
Borrow Wood Junior School, Spondon

Happiness

Happiness is yellow like the beautiful sun.
Happiness sounds like the whole world giggling and having fun.
Happiness tastes like a freshly made iced bun.
Happiness looks like the whole world is smiling and getting
on together.
Happiness feels like a soft pillow stuffed with feathers and
everything soft.
Happiness reminds me of happy times!

Jessica Kelly (10)
Borrow Wood Junior School, Spondon

Darkness

Darkness is as black as the void in space
Darkness is as quiet as the wind blowing in my face on a clear
summer's day
Darkness tastes like a kiwi curled up in its shell
It looks like the darkness of my room in the middle of the night
Darkness feels like a little baby chicken curled up in its egg
Darkness reminds me of the pitch-black of the night.

Ashley Cooper (10)
Borrow Wood Junior School, Spondon

Darkness

Darkness is the colour of a blackbird soaring high in the sky on
a winter's night.
Darkness sounds as silent as a mother bird landing on her nest
of baby chicks.
Darkness tastes like plain, mouldy old chocolate not eaten for 3 days.
It looks like someone asleep in a black room on a dark winter's night.
It feels like nobody in the world is able to love you as soon as
you are born.
Darkness reminds me of being lost in a world I don't know of.

Jayde Curry (10)
Borrow Wood Junior School, Spondon

Laughter

Laughter is yellow like buttercups when you are playing in
the garden.
Laughter sounds like the sea splashing on the rock on a
hot summer's day.
Laughter tastes like a strong lemon ice cream trickling down
your throat.
Laughter looks like a roller coaster going round and round.
Laughter feels like you are being tickled all over inside.
Laughter reminds me of a hot summer day on the beach.

Lauren Birkhead (10)
Borrow Wood Junior School, Spondon

Happiness

Happiness is the colour of a brown horse galloping in the sun.
Happiness is as loud as the marching band playing their instruments
in the middle of London.
Happiness tastes like a tropical cold ice lolly on a hot summer's day.
Happiness looks like a newborn puppy playing with its new toy.
Happiness feels like when you have not seen your friend in ages
and you have a laugh.
Happiness reminds me of going to the movies and spending time
with your family.

Liam Broad (10)
Borrow Wood Junior School, Spondon

Silence

Silence is as grey as a pigeon in town on a hot summer day.
Silence is as quiet as a classroom through the holidays,
sitting alone and still.
Silence is a tasty apple picked freshly from the tree this morning.
Silence looks like dark empty cupboard left getting dusty,
dark and forgotten.
Silence reminds me of a hot, breezy, dawning day
sitting on the beach alone watching as the sun dawns
and the sea rolls in and out very slowly and quietly.

Ashleigh McKenna (10)
Borrow Wood Junior School, Spondon

Jobs

Some people like cooking,
Some like hairdressing
And others like building.
I love teaching horse riding.

Megan Corlett (9)
Cranberry Junior School, Alsager

Dogs

Dogs are gorgeous, dogs are cute.
They love to be pampered.
They're always hyper and happy.
They are always ready to love you.

Annie Tyson (9)
Cranberry Junior School, Alsager

As I Walk Outside

As I walk outside I feel the wind blowing on my cold cheeks.
As I walk outside I see the children running to their friends.
As I walk outside I enjoy the playground full of toys and children.
As I walk outside I like everything outside.
As I walk outside.

Kieran Tucker (9)
Cranberry Junior School, Alsager

The World

Environmental disaster,
Illness,
Pollution,
Heat waves,
Noisy,
Dirty,
Tidal waves,
Tornadoes,
Hurricanes,
The world's a mess,
But it's my home!

Anna Weatherburn (9)
Cranberry Junior School, Alsager

Colours

Shimmering orange of the tropical sunset.
Blazing blue for the soft sea.
Pouncing pink for the pretty shells.
Gorgeous green for the wavy palm trees.
Young yellow for the shining sand.

Rachael Ayre (9)
Cranberry Junior School, Alsager

Kittens On A Cloud

What's the cutest thing in the world?
Kittens on a cloud,
Kittens on a cloud,
Soft and silky drinking milk,
Miaow, miaow, miaow.

She purrs up my leg,
She always begs,
She sits on her mat
And that is my cat.

Eden Lily Tagg (9)
Cranberry Junior School, Alsager

The Whole Wide World

The sea,
The sky,
The grass,
The birds that sing,
The morning sun that's awakening,
Everything you see is the whole wide world,
The sea,
The sky,
The grass,
The fish that swim,
The moonlight shining but it's very dim,
Everything you see and hear,
Everything you smell,
Everything around you is the whole wide world!

Chloe King (9)
Cranberry Junior School, Alsager

Morning

In the morning I am a sleepyhead,
But I still get out of bed.
I rush downstairs,
I bump my head,
I have breakfast
Then lie in bed watching TV
Until my mum says, 'Come and do your teeth.'
I do my teeth,
I wash my face,
But first of all I pull a funny face.
I tiptoe downstairs
And my brother gives me a glare
And then we have a dare.
We walk to school,
My brother falls over,
I pull him up,
He pulls me down.
We're at school, we're there
And the teacher says, 'Turn around!'

Joshua Arthurs (9)
Cranberry Junior School, Alsager

Magic

Magic is dangerous
Magic is bright
It is good but it can turn you into a kite
You must turn right and if something is black
It could turn white
So you must not go near the bright magic.

Adam Williams (9)
Cranberry Junior School, Alsager

In My Magic Tree

(Inspired by 'Magic Box' by Kit Wright)

I will put in my tree . . .

A splash of perfume on this night,
A horse that is white
And a colouring book to play with.

I will put in my tree . . .

A deep blue sea,
Smell of the air,
The sand slipper down my hand.

I will stick flowers in my tree,
I will make it go dark green,
I will make it into my own tree house.

Nicole Riach
Fieldhead Junior School, Birstall

The Magic Bone

(Inspired by 'Magic Box' by Kit Wright)

I will put in my bone . . .

The slime from a Boxer's mouth,
A hair from an elephant's trunk,
A tooth from an ancient grandpa.

I will put in my bone . . .

A skeleton with a moulting foot,
A witch with a wolf's cackle,
A devil with the grittiest nose.

I will put in my bone . . .

A blossom tree with a baby's skin,
Horses up every road,
Words that will always rhyme.

I will put in my bone . . .

A sound of a slivering snake,
A sound of a thin sausage
And a book with a teacher's voice.

I will put in my bone . . .

A teacher as a student,
A person on glasses
And a dog walking a human.

My bone is fashionable
With glitter and golden on the top
And at the sides wrapper with bones on it.

My bone is full.
In a few years' time
I will open it up and think.

Chloe-Louise Parkinson (10)
Fieldhead Junior School, Birstall

The Magic Treasure Chest

(Inspired by 'Magic Box' by Kit Wright)

I will put in the magic treasure chest . . .

A starfish that can talk to you
And a wish that will come true
What should I do?
A dog that likes to play
In a log, but he's a very funny dog
A key that will gleam and glow for a show.

Sophie Manning (10)
Fieldhead Junior School, Birstall

The Magic Castle

(Inspired by 'Magic Box' by Kit Wright)

I will put in the castle . . .

A magic key that will glow in the dark
A magic pencil case that can talk
And it can change colour in the night-time

I will put in the castle . . .

A magic key that can walk
A magic key that can sing to me
A magic bed that can fly

I will put in the castle . . .

A magic rubber that can fly
A magic parrot that can fly and talk
A magic cat that can lay gold eggs

I will put in the castle . . .

A magic book that can run
A magic pen that can lay red eggs.

Amy Leigh Hemingway (10)
Fieldhead Junior School, Birstall

The Magic Chest

(Inspired by 'Magic Box' by Kit Wright)

In my magic chest I will put . . .

A golden eagle soaring through the sky
A flying car that can talk
A talking speedboat that can walk

I will put in my chest . . .

A walking skateboard
A witch driving a flying saucer
And an alien flying a broomstick
The smell of pizza in a pizza joint

My chest is fashioned from metal, silver and aluminium
The hinges are the teeth of a crocodile
Crystals are in every corner
Sapphires everywhere
I will fly on the back of my chest and land on a sandy beach.

David Taylor (8)
Fieldhead Junior School, Birstall

The Magic Car

(Inspired by 'Magic Box' by Kit Wright)

I will put in the car . . .

A letter that can talk
Some keys that can stretch
A seat that can drive on a summer's day
The engine that can turn different colours

I will put in the car . . .

A pair of glasses that can move
A radio that can dance

I will put in the car . . .

A steering wheel that sings
A brake that can steer itself

My car is fashioned from gold and red and steal
With people on the top and secrets in the corners

I will surf in my car.

Sara Jane O'Brien (9)
Fieldhead Junior School, Birstall

Magic Mansion

(Inspired by 'Magic Box' by Kit Wright)

I will put in my mansion . . .

A gold smiling star in the sky shining on me,
A peaceful baby sleeping,
A blue dragon called Gyrados sweeping through the sky.

I will put in my mansion . . .

Eyes that pop out of your ears,
A zebra with blue stripes.
An alien waving hello,
A sunbathing dog,
A pen that does all your homework.

I will put in my mansion . . .

An old man's boot
Sweaty socks all around
A jumper monster

My mansion is fashioned with crystals round the door
And ruby emeralds,
Sapphires on the rooftop and pearl doorknobs
And a diamond remote to bring me back safe,
Sweet baby monsters roaming around the mansion
And a guard dragon at the front door blowing fire at intruders.

Joe Walsh (9)
Fieldhead Junior School, Birstall

My Magic Trophy

(Inspired by 'Magic Box' by Kit Wright)

I will put in my trophy . . .

Silver slime from a sea snail
An ancient man's toenail
A fifty foot-long beard

I will put in my trophy . . .

A magic carpet that can fly
Some banana boots
Frogs that can fly

I will put in my trophy . . .

An alien on a horse
A cowboy in a flying saucer
A fifth season with a green moon

I will put in my trophy . . .

The steam of saucy sausages
Tennis bats that can run
A skateboard that can run.

Bradley Parkes (9)
Fieldhead Junior School, Birstall

The Magic Chest

(Inspired by 'Magic Box' by Kit Wright)

I will put in my chest . . .

The sound of slivering snakes starved
The smell of cloudy chlorine

I will put in my chest . . .

The buzzing sound of bees
The eyesight of sweet suspicious swallows

I will put in my chest . . .

A car that wears glasses
An old man that wears headlights
A pen that wears a paper dress

My box is fashioned with secret voice codes
The hinges are made of the nails of a dinosaur
Now I have put all those things in
I will bury it and come back to it in a year or two.

Kendell Lucy Doyle (9)
Fieldhead Junior School, Birstall

The Magic Bone!

(Inspired by 'Magic Box' by Kit Wright)

I will put in my magic bone . . .

The slime from a dog's mouth,
A hair from an elephant's trunk,
A toenail from an ancient grandpa.

I will put in my magic bone . . .

A skeleton with a moulting skull,
A witch with a wolf's howl
And a wolf with a witch's cackle,
A devil with a snotty nose.

I will put in my magic bone . . .

A gremlin with a baby's bottom,
Horses on every street,
Words that always rhyme.

I will put in my magic bone . . .

The sound of a slithoring snake,
The swish of a tremendous tall tree,
The sound of the sea splashing onto the rocks.

My bone is fashioned with glitter everywhere
And on the top is fashioned with sparkling stones
That always smile at you, the pocket is decorated with gold.

My bone is full now, I will close it and in a few weeks' time
I will open it and empty it and fill it up again.

Lorraine Sherwood (9)
Fieldhead Junior School, Birstall

The Magic Bottle

(Inspired by 'Magic Box' by Kit Wright)

In my bottle I'll put . . .

A spell of a witch
A horse that's purple
A dino with pups
A fox with eggs

In my bottle I'll put . . .

The sound of a slithering snake
Blood of each first born
A sup of the deepest ocean in the world
A drink of the most beautiful lake there can be

In my bottle I'll put . . .

A smell of each beautiful flower
Dino toes and lots, lots more
In my magic bottle

With my bottle I'll show the world
So they can see the magic inside.

Danielle Taylor (9)
Fieldhead Junior School, Birstall

Thunderstorm

Lightning strikes with a *boom bang boom,*
The grey dark sky,
Tricks the lights of the night,
The lightning strikes at the trees,
The wind blows the people over,
The rain wets the fire out,
Move to where the lightning doesn't strike.

Charlie Price (8)
Meadows Primary & Nursery School, Ketley

Thunderstorm

When the thunder hits the ground
It makes a booming sound.
The clouds are grey,
Like the bay on a dull day.
The waves go high like they can fly.
The whistling wind blows and blows.

Kelsey Cadwallader (8)
Meadows Primary & Nursery School, Ketley

Thunderstorm Poem

As lightning strikes the ground,
I hate that horrible sound.
With a *boom, boom, bash,*
Lightning strikes the trash,
When the howling wind starts blowing,
That's when I really get scared,
The sky turns grey to black,
I want it to turn it back.

Hayley Fergusson (7)
Meadows Primary & Nursery School, Ketley

Thunderstorm

Lightning flashing in the sky
Thunder groaning on the sea
Windy roars swaying the trees
Rainy days of the week
Cloudy grey sky cooling the chimneypots
We're all unhappy because of the grey black sky.

Sam Henry (8)
Meadows Primary & Nursery School, Ketley

Thunderstorm

Dark black sky,
Lightning flashes up high,
Rain splashes in puddles,
Splish, splosh, splish
Wind howls at the door
Thunder crashes
Bang, boom, bang.

Katie Cresswell (8)
Meadows Primary & Nursery School, Ketley

Thunderstorm

The big, bold and black clouds in the sky
and the lightning goes by in the night sky,
the rain and the wind go together
and all around us we are surrounded
by the wind and rain.

Samantha Griffiths (8)
Meadows Primary & Nursery School, Ketley

Thunderstorm

Dark grey sky
When lightning hits the ground
Boom bang boom splash
Raindrops falling from the sky
The sky turns from blue to grey
Boom, thunder rumbling in the sky
Whoosh, the wind rattling the doors
Boats crashing on the shore
The great watery sea.

Lewis Rigby (8)
Meadows Primary & Nursery School, Ketley

What Is A Cloud?

A cloud is a big pillow for the sun to rest its head
A cloud is a soft white football kicked high in the sky
A cloud is a woolly lamb playing in the field
A cloud is a sheet of white paper drifting through a blue tunnel.

Jake Bradshaw (10)
Meadows Primary & Nursery School, Ketley

The Bonfire Creature

Jumping flames glowing red
Cracking noises that hurt your head

A monster dancing in the dark
A pile of burning leaves and bark

Smoke and ashes dance in the air
Bangs and cracks turn like a flare.

Luke Cadwallader (10)
Meadows Primary & Nursery School, Ketley

Friendship

F ab friend always look out for each other
R elationship is important to carry with your friends
I nside your heart, deep down, you are carrying love with
your friends
E very day you are having fun with your friends
N ever give up on your friends because deep down you care
D eep down you care and you are carrying love everywhere
S ophie is my friend and we get on and we carry love everywhere
H urting people's feelings is not caring for others
I nside you do care, make sure you show it
P roper friends carry love everywhere.

Tammy Woodman (11)
Meadows Primary & Nursery School, Ketley

Summer

Summer's great, summer's fun
We can play until the day is done
We bounce and roll
And graze our knees
But best of all we do as we please!

Ice cream man rolls down the hill
Playing music louder still
Money jingling inside our pockets
'What flavour love?'
'I want a rocket.'

As it gets colder
Fun draws to an end
There's still next year
So I suppose it's
Goodbye my friend.

Vicky Pope (10)
Meadows Primary & Nursery School, Ketley

The Blob

And . . . what is it like?

Oh, it's scary and fat-lumped
and spike-eared and moany.
It's hairy and face-grumped
and spotty and bony.

And . . . where does it live?

Oh, in rock lands and sea holes
and deserts and mountain tops.
In caves and in South Poles
and trees and cloud tops.

And . . .what does it eat?

Oh, dead flowers and turtle legs
and X-rays and moon crust.
Then burnt meat and sun-eggs
and lava and space dust.

And . . . what does it wear?

Not a thing. It's bare!

Sophie Banks (10)
Meadows Primary & Nursery School, Ketley

Smugglers

I have read a book about smugglers
And the exciting things they did
About the goods they smuggled
And the caves where they hid.

I think I'd be a good smuggler
For they sneak in and out
I could sneak up and down
I could creep and crawl about

I'm going to look in the paper
Where they advertise each week
I'm going to be a smuggler
I'm going to creep and sneak!

Sophie-Jane Hodgkinson (10)
Meadows Primary & Nursery School, Ketley

What Is The Sun?

The sun is a hot, round blazing fireball
that's been beamed into the sky.

The sun is a big yellow face
that's stuck down a drain in Heaven.

The sun is a big bouncy ball
that has been rolled across the sky.

The sun is a light bulb
screwed into a beautiful blue lampshade.

The sun is a yellow beach ball
kicked high into the summer sky.

Liam Norton (10)
Meadows Primary & Nursery School, Ketley

The Mystery

They dwell on a planet not far from the sun,
Some fly through outer space while others just run.
Some have big heads as hairless as tin,
While others have hair which sprouts from their skin.
Some dig moon crust and gobble this for meat,
The young squeal like pigs if you tickle their feet.
They slurp, burp, grunt, their manners are bad,
Their eyes become waterfalls when they feel sad.
Well who are these creatures, can you guess who?
The answer is simple, it's you, you and you!

Charlotte Adams (10)
Meadows Primary & Nursery School, Ketley

What Is A Million . . .

The grass growing on your back lawn.
The words you have read since you were born.

The green leaves on ten tall trees,
The number of times you have said please.

The amount of papers my teacher has marked,
The amount of cars I have seen parked.

The people met since you started school,
The water drops needed to fill the pool.

Jashan Bahad (9)
Meadows Primary & Nursery School, Ketley

What Is A Cloud?

It is a fluff of sheep fur sailing along a big blue pond.
It is a piece of candyfloss in a big blue bowl.
It is a fluffy pillow resting on a vast blue bed.
It is a white sponge in a big bucket of bright water.
It is a white floorboard where angels softly tread.
It is a soft white bed for people to rest on in Heaven.

Elliot Sharp (9)
Meadows Primary & Nursery School, Ketley

The Clouds Are Like

A cloud is like floating candyfloss.
A cloud is like a white sponge.
A cloud is like a bouncy castle.
A cloud is like a balloon.
A cloud is like cotton wool.
A cloud is like the sun's pillow.
The clouds are the gates to Heaven.

Connor J Kertland (10)
Meadows Primary & Nursery School, Ketley

What Is A Million?

The words that you've learnt since you were three,
The tricks that a pro has learnt in PE.

The hours that passed since you were born,
The sunrises since the sun was born.

The number of trees outside the school,
The drops of chlorine in the pool.

The number of times a manager has fired,
The number of metres ran before an athlete gets tired.

Calvin Edwards (10)
Meadows Primary & Nursery School, Ketley

What Is A Cloud?

A cloud is like candyfloss,
Searching for things you have lost.

A cloud is like a baby's blanket,
Wrapping its arms around its mother.

A cloud is like Heaven's earth,
Stepping towards a gate of flowers.

A cloud is like an island,
Miles away from anywhere.

Sophie Leigh Crompton (9)
Meadows Primary & Nursery School, Ketley

Children's Prayer

Let the teachers in our school
Not demand or try and act cool,
Clean our shoes until dawn,
Let us poke them with a thorn
Let us rule until the end of school
And Lord please, please can we have a swimming pool?

Let the teachers in our care
Let us play a spooky dare,
Let us have lots to drink,
But not make us have to think,
Not very tired or loud,
Or not as giant as a cloud.
Not make us write on the board,
Please, please *help us Lord!*

Matthew Jones
Meadows Primary & Nursery School, Ketley

Children's Prayer

Let the teachers in our school
Not be rude and not be cruel;
Let them not scream and shout
And let them not sing about!

Sack the teachers that spit and splutter,
Let them not hit and mutter,
Let the teachers run away
And let the children play all day.

Let the children hypnotise
All the teachers for a prize;
Let us learn, what we want
Burn the uniform because it's junk.

Harry Jones (10)
Meadows Primary & Nursery School, Ketley

Please Miss Riddell

(Based on 'Please Mrs Butler' by Allan Ahlberg)

Please Miss Riddell
This boy John Moo
Keeps copying my work Miss
What shall I do?

Go and sit outside dear
Take your books to the sink
Go and sit in class 11
Do whatever you think

Please Miss Riddell
This boy John Moo
Keeps taking my pencil Miss
What shall I do?

Keep it in your pencil pot
Hide it up your vest
Swallow it if you like my dear
Do what you think is best

Please Miss Riddell
This boy John Moo
Keeps pinching me Miss
What shall I do?

Lock yourself in a cupboard my dear
Go out to sea
Go out to a different country
But don't ask me!

Kieran Ursin-Smith (10)
Meadows Primary & Nursery School, Ketley

Please Mrs Butler

(Based on 'Please Mrs Butler' by Allan Ahlberg)

Please Mrs Butler
This boy Derek Drew
Keeps looking at me funny Miss
What shall I do?

Go and sit in the park dear
Go and do your test
Take your work to the mayor my love
Do whatever you think is best

Please Mrs Butler
This boy Derek Drew
Keeps poking me on my back Miss
What shall I do?

Go on the roof my lamb
Go and sit at my desk.
Take it to the headmaster love
Just get on with your test

Please Mrs Butler
This boy Derek Drew
Keeps copying my work Miss
What shall I do?

Go and sit in the sink dear
Run away to sea
Do whatever you want to do
But don't ask *me!*

Amanda Jones (10)
Meadows Primary & Nursery School, Ketley

Night, Night

Night, night,
Moonlight shining, showing secrets,
Night, night,
People dreading its darkness.

Night, night,
Owls hooting, wolves howling,
Night, night,
Snakes slithering, bugs staring.

Night, night,
Crowded, noisy, everything still,
Night, night,
Trees mistaken for scary shapes.

Night, night,
Sun is rising, dawn is coming,
Night, night,
Is chased away - it will be light for the rest of today.

Blake Prince (11)
Meadows Primary & Nursery School, Ketley

Vulture

As quick as an eagle,
soaring through the air,
searching with eyes like fire,
looking for a carcass, old or rare.

Wings flash out, gliding through the sky,
beak sharp and ready,
to tear away flesh, ready,
steady, *gooo!*

Diving down deep, like jumping into water,
talons alarmed and prepared to seize,
land on soft ground and sprint towards prey,
holding on tight to it, like gripping onto a trapeze.

Fighting off visitors can be quite hard,
but not for a vulture,
peck them, bite them so they will go
and look at *your* carcass - as delicate as a sculpture.

That's it now,
you've won the fight,
so warn the intruders,
because they'll get a fright.

Paige Mansell (11)
Meadows Primary & Nursery School, Ketley

My Favourite Team!

Come on Liverpool,
I know you are the best,
Even if my mates say no,
You're better than the rest!

You can win the FA Cup,
I know you can,
I trust you a lot,
I'm your biggest fan!

Steven Gerrard, you're the best,
Dad agrees with me,
He also loves Jamie Carragher,
That's who I want to be!

Rafa Benitez is fantastic,
The fans are great,
Shouting, screaming and singing,
'We are your mates!'

I love you Liverpool!

Laura Jade Pye (11)
Meadows Primary & Nursery School, Ketley

My Aunt's Dogs

My aunt has a dog called Stan,
Who plays all day with a rusty old pan,
He has brown and white fur
And is mostly a blur,
No wonder he's started to purr.

My aunt has a dog called Millie,
Who had a little friend called Lillie.
She came over one day,
With her friend Tilly May,
I wonder why they didn't stop and play.

My aunt has a dog Ben,
Who always clucks like a hen,
But when it gets dark,
He always barks,
I wonder what happens by day.

Natasha Evans (10)
Meadows Primary & Nursery School, Ketley

Homework

Lessons in school are normally boring,
Especially when they are in the morning.

One day in class we started a new topic. . . trees
'I would rather sail the sea than do this boring subject about
trees and green leaves.'

But the lesson turned out rather funny,
We were discussing trees when suddenly
The teacher asked, 'Roann! think of a sentence with sycamore in.'
This is where the fun begins!
I thought for a second then I replied,
'I am sycamore homework I can't cope with it all the time.'

The teacher was not impressed,
She gave me a funny look,
But I started to laugh,
So I covered my face with a book.

Roann Tracey (11)
Meadows Primary & Nursery School, Ketley

Seasons

Winter

Cold, freezing, white as snow
Cold, freezing, watch your face glow
See snowdrops landing on your nose

Spring

Leaves, leaves grow all day
Flowers, flowers come out to play
So come, come and play all day

Summer

Dance, dance in the sun
Come, come and have some fun

Autumn

Leaves, leaves come off the trees
Jump, jump on the count of *three!*

Hannah Beaman (10)
Meadows Primary & Nursery School, Ketley

Night

Night is death,
Swallowing the sun.
Nine o'clock,
It has just begun.

Night is hell,
Turning everything black.
The darkness creeps in,
Every rock and gloomy crack.

Night is transforming
Into day.
My favourite time
Is when night fades away.

I lie in bed,
The night has gone.
I stare at the wall,
Where the moon once shone.

It is now midday,
But I am still afraid.
I am afraid of dusk,
Where the ghostly night waits.

Kieran Smart (11)
Meadows Primary & Nursery School, Ketley

The Eagle

He flaps his golden, long wings in the sky,
Close to the sun, he's really high.
Stretches his claws through the air,
Catching his prey quick as a flash.

Watching on the mountain walls,
Spying on the town halls,
And like a thunderbolt he falls.

Courteney Williams (10)
Meadows Primary & Nursery School, Ketley

The Golden Beach

Soft, glistening, golden sand
Melting ice cream in my hand.

Crashing waves on the rocks,
Soft sand in my socks.

Beautiful colourful flowers
Sparkling in the scorching sun for hours.

Grass waving in the cool breeze
Saying hello to the swaying trees.

Ruth Bethany Beaman (8) & Abder Rahman (9)
Meadows Primary & Nursery School, Ketley

The Moon

The moon is like sparkly footballs
A floating bubble in space,
A shimmery boulder drifting in space
A floating round piece of glass in the night.

The moon is like a shiny polished pebble
A round piece of tinsel in the dead dark sky
A circular rock flying in outer space
An empty plate hovering in outer space.

Phillip Shepherd (9)
Meadows Primary & Nursery School, Ketley

The Shiny Moon

The moon is like a cold ball.
The moon is like a cold shiny ball.
Just laying there
Covered in glitter and shiny tinsel.
The moon is like a sparkly ball.

The moon is like a glittery ball.
The moon is like a round football being
Kicked by a mysterious space alien.

The moon is like a ball.
The moon is like a giant's face
Surrounded in a sea of stars.

Callum Locke (9)
Meadows Primary & Nursery School, Ketley

Shining Sun

A hot sparkling sun blazes in the boiling air
with the clear blue sky.

It shimmers above us, bringing light
to the world.

Daniel Naylor (7)
Meadows Primary & Nursery School, Ketley

The Moon Is Like . . .

The moon is like a spinning football floating in the sky,
The moon is like a big bumpy bubble floating in the sky.
Like a big silver rocket surrounded by stars.

Shona Ward (8)
Meadows Primary & Nursery School, Ketley

Summer Morning

A bright blazing sun,
All the children are having fun.
Sand tickling me between my toes,
The sun is sparkling on the blue sea
As it flows.

Tanasorn Thaku (8)
Meadows Primary & Nursery School, Ketley

The Moon

The moon is like a pale silver bauble
hanging on a Christmas tree and shining out in the sunless night.
Flying into space, looking like a round sparkling rocket,
spreading tinsel over the darkness in the sky.

The moon is like a shining, sparkling ball
being kicked through space,
Sailing high up in the air, spreading glistening glitter
from high up in the sky.
The moon is like a polished pebble floating in the dusty
dark night, up high in the sky.
Spreading clear-as-crystal water
all over the world.

Rowan Jones (8)
Meadows Primary & Nursery School, Ketley

The Sparkling Moon

The moon is like a clock face on the wall in the winter's night,
The moon is white and sparkly, floating in the dark sky.

The moon glistens around the sky,
It is like a black playground,
The moon is spinning and spinning in the sky.

The sparkly moon is like a light bulb hanging on a thread of stars.
Shiny silver is the moon, sparkling round in the sky.
The moon is bright.

Megan Tibbetts (8)
Meadows Primary & Nursery School, Ketley

The Moon Poem

The moon is like a sparkling shooting star,
It shines in the night sky.
The moon is like a floating bubble in the darkness.
The moon is like a sparkling bauble on a Christmas tree,
It shines in space.
The moon is like a light bulb hanging on a thread of stars.
A polished pebble floating in the dark sky.
The moon spins around like a shiny disco ball.

Rachel Williams (8)
Meadows Primary & Nursery School, Ketley

Monday's Child

Monday's child eats loads of chilli,
Tuesday's child is really silly,
Wednesday's child stays up late,
Thursday's child opens the gate,
Friday's child likes loads of pips,
Saturday's child moves her lips,
But the child that is born on the Sabbath day
Is the one that loves each and every day.

Chloe Norton (7)
Meadows Primary & Nursery School, Ketley

Monday's Child

Monday's child likes to dream,
Tuesday's child likes ice cream,
Wednesday's child likes to act,
Thursday's child has a contract,
Friday's child saw a unicorn,
Saturday's child found an acorn,
But the child that is born on the Sabbath day
Is good and rich and gets their own way.

Molly Banks (8)
Meadows Primary & Nursery School, Ketley

Why It's Good To Be Me

I'm caring and kind
And very energetic.
I have a sharp mind,
My life's very hectic!

It's good to be me because
I have great friends.
I like my school
Because it helps me learn.

I have great parents,
They love me so much.
That's why *it's good to be me!*

Scott Sobanja (11)
Meadows Primary & Nursery School, Ketley

The Dark Streets

Upon the dark streets
Of the city lanes,
Creatures rummage around
In bins and drains.

Birds and bats
Fly through the air,
Cold and dark,
Without a care.

Cat flaps flip
As they open and close,
Because the cats are going to sleep
At the time of no one knows.

Upon the dark streets
Of the city lanes,
Creatures rummage around
In bins and drains.

Jessica Banks (11)
Meadows Primary & Nursery School, Ketley

Sam, Sam The Funny Old Man

Sam, Sam the funny old man
Washed his face in a clean frying pan.
He combed his hair with a horse's tail
And scratched his neck with his big toenail.

Sam, Sam the funny old man,
Lost his frying pan.
He cried and he coughed
Until he turned soft.

Sam, Sam the funny old man,
Found his frying pan.
He laughed and smiled
Until he went wild.

Sarah Pidgeon (11)
Meadows Primary & Nursery School, Ketley

Bullies

B ullies are everywhere
U nderstand what they do
L eave the bullies behind
L et your teacher know
I nclude your family
E xplain what happened
S mile when it's over.

John Pidgeon (8)
Meadows Primary & Nursery School, Ketley

Life Of A Fairy

I come in the night
When lights are bright,
My wings they sparkle with such delight.
Around your room I fly so free,
Wishing you would be with me.
The life of a fairy is so much fun,
I don't have to walk, skip, run,
So in your dreams, think of me
When you're there lying in your bed at night.
I like you, sleeping when you turn out the light.

Emily Whitehouse (9)
Meadows Primary & Nursery School, Ketley

My Friends

I have loads of friends at school,
They think I'm really cool.
We love to go out and play
On a really sunny day.

My best friend's name is Kelly,
She loves eating jelly.
Kelly is my best friend,
Our friendship will never end.

Shelley Fergusson (9)
Meadows Primary & Nursery School, Ketley

Honey And Tigger

I have a cat and dog,
Their names are Tigger and Honey.
Tigger is very lazy
And Honey is very funny.
I take Honey for a walk
And she likes to jump around,
But Tigger likes to lie in the sun
And doesn't make a sound.

Heather Felton (9)
Meadows Primary & Nursery School, Ketley

Moon

A crystal-white, banana moon,
She will come to see you soon.
As wise as a smile,
A big orange pile.

She glides across,
She is the boss,
That's why they
Call her the moon.

She is silver and gold,
We think she's old,
Just because
We are children.

Lauryn Hayward (8)
Meadows Primary & Nursery School, Ketley

Man United, The Champions

We rarely lost,
We always won
And we have our hands
On the only one.

The Premiership is
There for all,
You cannot afford to slip,
Or you will fall.

Chelsea, Liverpool, Arsenal
Are some of the rest,
But Manchester United
Are the best.

Niall O'Sullivan (9)
Meadows Primary & Nursery School, Ketley

Softly Sound

When the wind blows,
The trees bend and creak.
When the rain falls,
The rivers become extra deep.

When the snow flutters,
The fields are covered in white.
When the sun shines,
The sky is so bright.

Alice Keay (9)
Meadows Primary & Nursery School, Ketley

Spike, The Dog

Most dogs like to run around,
Bury their bones in the ground,
But Spike doesn't, he likes
Chewing the wallpaper, ripping up old shoes,
That's what Spike is like.
Is he like your dog?

Most dogs like to eat
Juicy chops of meat.
Crunchy biscuits, *crunch, crunch, crunch,*
To look through the junk,
But not Spike, oh no, he's an odd dog,
He likes to watch the BBC racing,
Chasing the cat next door
And scratching on the floor.
Is he like your dog? *Nooo way!*

Tia Price (8)
Meadows Primary & Nursery School, Ketley

The Lion

The lion is the king of the beasts,
He chews on meat of which he feasts.
In the African jungle they call him *Highness,*
Because of the way he roars out of his chest.
But I think that whatever the lion is,
I'd rather be somewhere else
Because of his enormous mouth!

Amy Dhillon (10)
Meadows Primary & Nursery School, Ketley

Monster Mayhem

What was that noise?
Was it one of my toys?
Upstairs in my room
There was a very loud boom
And I thought it was coming from my cupboard.

I opened the door,
There was a shake on the floor
And then a very loud roar.
What could it be?
I knocked my knee
On that dark slimy thing.

My heart was pumping,
It was getting faster and faster.
I reached out my arm
And grabbed the dark monster.
I screamed out loud
Like a noisy rain cloud
And then saw my mum come in.

She switched on the light
And I jumped with fright
And saw there was nothing there.

I looked on the floor
And saw by the door
That the dark monster
Was only my costume.

I laughed out loud and turned around
And saw a hand on my shoulder . . .
Argh! Monster mayhem!

Liam Hall (8)
Meadows Primary & Nursery School, Ketley

Like A . . .

I'm like a bird
Who soars in the sky.
I'm like a cat
Clever and sly.
I'm like a cheetah
Quick as can be.
I'm like a giraffe
Tall as a tree.
I'm like a snake
Slithering low.
I'm like a hamster
Trapped in a cage.
I'm like a lion
Roaring with rage.

Jessica Rogers (9)
Meadows Primary & Nursery School, Ketley

The Super Spy

There's a man in a boat with a black and white coat,
With a patch on his eye and a growl in his throat.
I hope it's not true that he's coming after you,
Look out, look out, look out because you don't know what he'll do.
I think we might discover that he is working undercover,
He won't let you die because he is a super spy.

Ashleigh-Jo Hodnett (9)
Meadows Primary & Nursery School, Ketley

The Journey

My motorbike is a ferocious beast
with a heart made of iron.
It prowls down the A52 like a cheetah
Hunting down a juicy delectable antelope.

The engine, a lion roaring,
Makes cars swerve out of its path.

But when a lorry is in the way,
The only thing this beast can do
Is wait until the gorilla moves out of its path.

In the quiet places of its destination,
This beast stops prowling,
And then goes to sleep.

Daniel Pilkington (11)
St Andrew's CE Primary School, Stanley

The Water

The water is extremely hot,
In the little circular pot,
It burns my hands,
It cooks my glands,
So it must be a very hot pot.

William Stanton (10)
St Andrew's CE Primary School, Stanley

My Journey To The South Of France

My car is like a house on wheels,
But much lighter than a house.
We zoom along the motorway
As fast as can be.

My car is melting in the sun
And it's melting me as well.
We keep on asking, 'Are we there yet?'
My dad says, 'Nearly.'

My car is going as slow as a turtle
Because we have hit a traffic jam.
The Tom Tom is driving me up the wall
Because it is ahead of time.

I have asked my dad if we are there yet,
He said, 'Yes, just one minute.'
Now the best part - putting up the tent,
The part my dad hates.

Shashannah Lamb (10)
St Andrew's CE Primary School, Stanley

An A-Z Of Terrific Transport

A eroplanes travel in the air
B uses queuing to get home
C ars beeping to get through
D riving on the road
E ngines roaring
F orever they go
'G et out of the way,' they say
H elicopters fly by
I can see them for miles
J ets zoom in the sky
K ayaks floating in the river
L imos come by
M ustangs red, all sorts of colours
N oise beeping from the cars
O pen the windows on the bus
P eople in their cars driving home
Q uads park for the day
R un away or the mustangs will run
                    over you, they go so fast
S tand clear of the cars
T raffic jams never-ending
U nder the bridge the trains go
V ehicles crashing into one another
W ait for people to cross
X anadu, the state of futuristic cars
Y oung people drive cars
Z ebra crossing, wait till the cars have gone by.

Lauren Broxholme (10)
St Andrew's CE Primary School, Stanley

The Journey

The train is a monster of movement,
A dragon upon the track,
Like a gigantic creature
Travelling through the black.

In the moonlit town,
Winding its way through the dark,
I sit drinking a cup of tea.
In the distance I hear a dog bark.

I hear the hoot of an owl,
I hear the toot of a train,
I hear the chugging on the rails,
But they all just sound the same.

My head is starting to hurt,
My eyelids start to fall,
The dragon seems to slowly stop,
It feels magical.

The dragon sighs a breath of smoke,
The sound's like a ride at the fair,
The beast starts his race again
without a single care.
Going, going, going . . . gone..

Bethany Morledge (10)
St Andrew's CE Primary School, Stanley

The Journey

The burly beast blows up its engine
And calls in the tiny servants to push
Out the monstrous machine from
The place of sleep.

'Let's go!' commands the engine
And up, up, up goes the burly beast
Into the air to reach its destination.

Whilst in the air, out comes their food,
The smell trickling up the passengers' noses,
Then eventually reaching their stomachs,
Everyone feeling their starvation.

Finally, the plane lands at the destination
And the wheels reach the runway,
And then the monster flits down the path.
The plane has a few hours' rest
And then the cycle restarts.

Connor Pooles (10)
St Andrew's CE Primary School, Stanley

My Car Journey

My car runs steadily on the smooth road,
When we go faster it gallops with the wind.
On the road it flows like a river,
The car boasting to go faster,
Sprinting like a cheetah in the desert,
It swerves through all the cars.
Out of the exhaust comes the smoke.
Slowly, softly down the town we go,
I drive up the road,
'Stop,' I say to my car.
I turn around, drive back to my house,
Then I leave my car on her own,
All tired and cold
And waiting to have another ride tomorrow.

Danielle Waddingham (10)
St Andrew's CE Primary School, Stanley

What Is The Sun?

The sun is a ball made of fire,
But in gold.
It shines brightly as we get into our cars,
Burning our bottoms
As we are seated.
Makes the effect of a beautiful rainbow
Because shining sun and boring rain
Will create a colourful rainbow.

Chloe Martin (10)
St Andrew's CE Primary School, Stanley

The Journey

When the plane is still
It looks like a bird
When it has been told
To stay motionless.
Then it rolls, like a bird
Running to get ready to fly.
The aeroplane goes up and up
Into the baby-blue sky.
She flies like a beautiful bird
Zooming away.

She is a bird when she
Goes through all the clouds
And soars through the sky.
She is a baby bird trying
To learn how to fly.

Chelsey Thomas (11)
St Andrew's CE Primary School, Stanley

A-Z Of Travelling Transport

A is for aeroplanes whizzing in the sky

B is for buses going up and down

C is for cars dashing down the road

D is for double-decker buses carrying more people than other buses

E is for engines letting transport work

F is for ferries taking you over the sea

G is for go-karts going round in circles

H is for hot air balloons lifting people off their feet

I is for ice cream vans giving out ice cream in a cone

J is for jets reaching the distance of 250km

K is for kayaks, boats with loads of seats

L is for lorries carrying goods for Christmas

M is for motorbikes darting down the motorway

N is for noisy traffic jams making people late for work

O is for Orville and Wilbur inventing the plane

P is for prams carrying babies backwards and forwards

Q is for quarries letting boats cross to places

R is for racing cars going to and fro

S is for ships taking you to different countries

T is for trains moving down the tracks

U is for unicycle with not three, not two, but one wheel

V is for Vauxhall car going up and down the streets

W is for warships battling the other team

X is for the xylophone chimes of the ice cream vans

Y is for yellow cars speeding across the road

Z is for zebra crossings letting people cross a road.

Jordan Stone (10)
St Andrew's CE Primary School, Stanley

What Is a Rainbow?

A rainbow is like a beautiful archway
In the sky.
A painting from the sun and rain.
A place where people think there is
A pot of gold at the end,
And fading away with the bright sun.
It is a walkway of imagination,
A headband full of colours on
The little girl's head,
Bright colours, dark colours and in-between colours.
Now we are watching this amazing rainbow
Fade away.

Amber Kelly (10)
St Andrew's CE Primary School, Stanley

The Journey

Waiting, waiting for the plane to take off,
Fasten your seatbelt, it is time to go.
Rumbling and grunting like a hungry hog,
Starting its engine ready to fly.
Off we go, with the wind whistling behind,
Soaring through the midday sky.
She is a bird with gleaming white feathers
Flying through the air.
She starts to lower,
The plane goes slower.
Down she goes,
It is time to rest.

Freya Turner (10)
St Andrew's CE Primary School, Stanley

The Steam Train

The slow tortoise train
Slowly went down the track,
Then suddenly, the train
Puffed a massive
Cloud of smoke.
The fast and furious train
Went speeding down the hill,
They were five miles
From the station.
The train
Eventually got to the station.

Jack Wagg (10)
St Andrew's CE Primary School, Stanley

What Is Fire?

Fire is like a lion's mane
Burning away in the sun.
Fire is like a dragon's fiery breath
Over the mountain tops.
Fire is like a droplet of the sun
Landing on the floor.

Jack Annable (10)
St Andrew's CE Primary School, Stanley

My Journey

There she is, soaring in the sky,
Engines propelling her from airport to airport.
The astonishing, fantastic flight of a life,
Rumbling and cluttering up the sky.
Here she is! She can really fly,
Having blades of steel,
Or carving knives.
Cutting the clouds as she hovers by,
As high as the sky, as low as the sea,
The mountain rescue team save me,
The clouds expanding, being cut all over.
There is a pilot like a heart of gold,
Telling her what to do.
And the bowl-like sea
Awaits the beast.
As she goes out of control,
Bashing and clashing in the ribbon sea.

Jack Briddon (11)
St Andrew's CE Primary School, Stanley

The Journey

I caught a train to my nana's,
It was like a roaring dragon
Panting for breath.
It was charging through
All through the cities.
It's like a non-stop cheetah
With wheels.
The seats were like a sofa,
As soft as a teddy bear.
I enjoyed the journey,
The coaches were like
A front room on wheels.
At the end of the journey
The train was like an
Out-of-breath cheetah of steel.

James Bailey (10)
St Andrew's CE Primary School, Stanley

Journey In A Car

The car waits for its owner by the garage door,
Waiting for morning, that's what it's for.
The journey of rampage until noon,
But she's not ready, it's full moon.
The owner's ready, it's time to go,
Past the villagers and say hello.
The window wiper behind is like
A dog wagging its tail,
This old girl could never fail!
Peugeot on the left, Ford on the right,
All the cars are in my sight.
Back home now, safe and sound,
The dog's so glad, that silly hound.

Samuel Holland (10)
St Andrew's CE Primary School, Stanley

The Journey

My legs scamper to power him,
Like a greyhound running
Swiftly through the terrain.
He stops for no one.
He flies right past you like a javelin.
My bike, a silver dart, it shoots right past you.

George Scowby (11)
St Andrew's CE Primary School, Stanley

An A-Z Travelling Transport

A eroplanes fly through the sky
B oat sailing across the sea
C ar driving down the road
D iggers digging up the ground
E ngines breaking down
F erry sailing across the sea
G o-karts racing round the track
H elicopters flying through the air
I nto the plane people go
J etpack shooting to the sky
K ayaks bump down the river
L imos speeding down the road
M otorbike racing down the street
N oisy police car racing past cars
O ops, went the wrong way
P assengers getting money
Q ueues getting bigger and bigger
R apids toss the boat
S ubmarine gliding underwater
T rains rushing across the tracks
U nderwater shipwrecks
V ehicles racing
W aiting for traffic lights
X -types
Y arises,
Z ebra crossing.

Harry Clarke (10)
St Andrew's CE Primary School, Stanley

Transport Alphabet

A udi R8s use their power to
B eat
C hryslers at
D rag races.
E volutions
F ight
G Ts even though they
H ave half the power.
I t's really good how
J aguars have
K eys that are
L ight
M etal.
N o, probably not.
O n the road
P ick-up trucks travel not very
Q uickly.
R iakkonen
S peeds
T hrough
U ndulating S-bends.
V olvos,
W estfields,
X -types and
Y arises
Z oom (or try to anyway).

Robert Palin (10)
St Andrew's CE Primary School, Stanley

My Boat Journey

When I get on a wobbly ferry,
It makes me feel excited.
I've got on the vacillating ferry
That is motionless to start with.
The ferry finally starts up
Whilst I'm finding my way
To a seat near a window.
As my bluey-coloured boat
Moves along the water,
She's like a water snail,
She's moving steadily along the sea.
My boat then gently glides
Into a storm,
However I think my beauty of a boat
Is seasick.
The storm has blown itself away,
Like blowing away leaves
In the garden.
The bluey water machine
Is almost at its destination,
However, I don't feel well.
I'm there now,
But I can't wait for my holiday
And my trip going back.

Adele Gibb (11)
St Andrew's CE Primary School, Stanley

The Journey

My car is as fast as a cheetah,
Speeding past the cameras at lightning speed.
The wheels on my car are like propellers on a helicopter,
Moving faster and faster.
Flames are coming out of my exhaust
Like a dragon breathing fire.

My car is painted like a cheetah sprinting down the track,
At lightning speed it shall yet go.
To break the fastest car record, going past all the tightest corners
And won't go off the track.
And now go home and have its nap.

Michael Daykin (10)
St Andrew's CE Primary School, Stanley

Untitled

There was a young lady of Ireland,
Who had a very almighty hand,
She needed large gloves
That were made from doves,
That impressive young lady of Ireland.

Jessica Hallam (11)
St Andrew's CE Primary School, Stanley

An A-Z Travelling Transport

A eroplane flying through the air
B oat sailing across the bumpy sea
C ars driving through the lanes
D rivers driving down the M1
E ngines breaking down
F erries taking people to any island
G o-karts giving little children rides
H elicopters going through the sky
I nto a hot air balloon people climb
J etpack shooting to the stars
K -Nines watch cars go speeding by
L imos taking important people to places
M otorbike speeding past lorries
N umber plates on a car
O h people are going the wrong way
P assengers are getting impatient
Q ueues growing bigger and bigger
R apids toss the boats upside down
S ubmarine sees the Great Barrier Reef
T rains go running by
U nderwater shipwrecks are homes for fish
V ehicles everywhere
W aterway rivers toss boats around
X tra fuel to keep us going
Y eah, the bus has finally arrived
Z ebra crossings guide people safely across the road.

Emily Lane (10)
St Andrew's CE Primary School, Stanley

School Trip

The school trip was a special occasion,
But we never reached our destination.
Instead of the zoo
I was locked in the loo
Of an M6 service station.

Isaac Hurst (8)
St Thomas Aquinas RC Primary School, Stoke-on-Trent

My Headmaster From A Dream

My headmaster gives you a trip to detention,
It's like he's doing it for a collection.
My headmaster has an office room,
Full of destruction, despair and doom!

My teacher gives you an icy glare,
That even a devil couldn't bear,
He gives you a stare in the eye
And he wears the most awful tie!

You hear him stomping down the hall,
He's really, really, *really* tall.
He is very chubby and enormously fat,
And he owns a vicious pet cat.

He has the most ugly face,
And he always carries a dark black case.
So be careful if he comes to your school,
Listen up and don't be a fool.

Brandan Broadhurst (10)
St Thomas Aquinas RC Primary School, Stoke-on-Trent

My Brother Will Do Everything

My brother will do everything,
just you wait and see.
He will climb the highest mountain
and catch a mighty shark.
He will swim in the giant wavy sea
and he will ride a hungry lion.
He will fight a ferocious dragon
and he will find the sweetest rose.
He will walk a thousand miles
and he will live in the jungle.
He will find the biggest shell.
You can see how my brother will do everything!

Laura Green (8)
St Thomas Aquinas RC Primary School, Stoke-on-Trent

A Sister Of Mine

M y sister is cute and cuddly
Y oung and always lovely

S he's cute but noisy
I love her lots
S o she's the best of all the tots
T ogether we play
E ach and every day
R ain or shine she will always be
  A sister of mine.

Alice Dudley (8)
St Thomas Aquinas RC Primary School, Stoke-on-Trent

My Family And Friends

I live with my mum,
She's a lot of fun.
I live with my dad
He's sometimes mad.
I live with my brother,
We love each other.
We're a great family.

My grandad Hill,
He'll cheer me up, yes he will!
My grandad Ted,
He used to have a horse, he said.
My dad's dad
He's never sad.
I love them all, oh yes.

My nanny Diane is great,
She has a daughter called Kate.
My nanny Val is very sweet,
She likes places tidy and neat.
We see Nanny Maud every Saturday,
We can visit when we want, that's what she'd say.
My two great nans I love very much
We try very hard to keep in touch.

My friends are great,
But Alice is my best mate.
Ellie and Isabella are lots of fun,
Florence really likes to run.
Millie talks to me a lot,
She's quite small, a little dot.

My friends and family are the best,
They will stick up for me and never rest.

Millie Walkaden (9)
St Thomas Aquinas RC Primary School, Stoke-on-Trent

My Riddle

My first is in melon but not in fruit
My second is in yacht but not in boat.
My third is in fast but not in slow
My fourth is in art and also in paint
My fifth is in Matthew and also in name
My sixth is in igloo and also in ice
My seventh is in Lego and also in blocks
My eighth is in yellow but not in colour.

What am I?

A: My family.

Mary Krystin Castro (8)
St Thomas Aquinas RC Primary School, Stoke-on-Trent

Seasons For All

Spring . . . When the sky turns blue,
The sun says *hello to you,*
Then a gentle breeze passes by,
Like a cuddle from the sky!

Summer . . . The rays of the sun are so hot,
Which makes flowers grow in their pot,
Then the children play outside,
Until it is time for this season to hide!

Autumn . . . The leaves change colour and that is all,
Then they slowly start to fall,
This is a great time, day and night,
You could not leave it out of your sight!

Winter . . . Winter, winter, snow, snow, snow,
Winter means a *ho, ho, ho!*
Even though the sun doesn't shine
Winter is still one of mine!

Marianne Hernandez (9)
St Thomas Aquinas RC Primary School, Stoke-on-Trent

Spring

S pring is my favourite time of year
P lants of spring are flowers and newborn baby lambs
R oses are red bluebells are blue
I love to see the daffodils blooming in spring
N ests of eggs and baby birds
G oats and lambs are being born in spring.

Georgina Davenhill (8)
St Thomas Aquinas RC Primary School, Stoke-on-Trent

Big Snugly Hugs

B ig hugs are lovely, big hugs make me happy
I love big hugs and I want one right now
G ive it to me now because I'm feeling very lonely

S uch a big hug that it squeezes all my insides out
N ever be rude in hugs, they always have to be brilliant
U tterly snug as a bug, snug as a mug, snug as hot chocolate
wrapped in a rug
G otta make your arms warm so I don't get chilly - give me room to
breathe though remember
L et me squeeze into the tiny chair in the corner of the room.
Y es, you'll make it snuggly, yes you'll make it warm but remember
it has to be from you

P lease, pretty please, I'm begging you, please
I would like it very special, just mine in fact, make it a world record
E verybody likes hugs, they make you feel cosy.

H elp me today by giving me a hug because I love it,
U npleasant things are not included in a hug, it's always perfect
G ive me a hug it will really make my day and when you're feeling
glum I'll give you ono.

Piper Everest (8)
St Thomas Aquinas RC Primary School, Stoke-on-Trent

A Family Poem

My mum is kind
My mum can be gentle
My mum also is careful
My mum is a good cook
Is that what you think too?

My sister is very cute
My sister can be cheeky
My sister is also silly
But most of all she is a crazy cat.

I am a chatterbox but very cute
I can be funny to make people laugh
I also can be very, very sneaky
But most of all I like being the way I am now
Which is *helpful!*

Lauren Read (8)
St Thomas Aquinas RC Primary School, Stoke-on-Trent

My Holiday Poem

D is for dancing in the night club at night,
E is for some of the exciting things you can do there
V is for very hot and sunny at the beach,
O is for orange juice, you can buy there
N is for *never* bored.

Hannah Benson (9)
St Thomas Aquinas RC Primary School, Stoke-on-Trent

Seasons

Seasons are great.

Winter so cold, dark and dreary,
But the snowman makes me cheery.
Winter, Santa comes,
Bang, bang on the drums.

Spring blossom popping out,
For I love spring no doubt.
Spring lambs are born,
In the early dawn.

Summer in the paddling pool,
Summer is so cool!
Summer holidays are here,
Let's jump and cheer.

Autumn leaves off trees,
Away go the bees.
The daylight does not last,
For it goes very fast.

Ben Oakes (7)
St Thomas Aquinas RC Primary School, Stoke-on-Trent

My Favourite Season

S easons are great and very much fun,
  especially in autumn because the food
  is really really, yum-yum!
E veryone likes it when it's summer
  but I like autumn.
A fter the storm, I like to play in the
  autumn every day.
S ometimes I play on autumn days
  but I also like to play.
O ver the river there are autumn trees
  surrounded by lots of bees.
N obody knows what I am saying but I have
  to go and see you next time in the autumn,
  when all the flowers grow.

Tadi Munyanyi (8)
St Thomas Aquinas RC Primary School, Stoke-on-Trent

My Sister

Sometimes I like her,
Sometimes I don't,
She can be lovely,
And sometimes she's not.

But she's my sister,
I love her so,
I want to hold her
And never let her go.

I never want her to leave me,
I hope she never will,
She is my best friend,
I know that I'm hers.

She is so beautiful,
Happy and kind,
Thank you God for making her
And making her mine.

Connor Declan Thomas (8)
St Thomas Aquinas RC Primary School, Stoke-on-Trent

Friends

F riends help and care for you,
R ain or sun, your friends are always there for you.
I nclude different people in your games.
E njoy different times with your friends.
N obody wants to be lonely.
D ifferent people mean different friendships.
S mile, don't be grumpy.

Isabella Dawson (9)
St Thomas Aquinas RC Primary School, Stoke-on-Trent

My Favourite Thing - Dalek

There once was a nine year old Dalek,
Who was allergic to garlic,
First he went *bang!*
Then he went *twang!*
Ended up in the castle of Harlech.

Robert Shenton (10)
St Thomas Aquinas RC Primary School, Stoke-on-Trent

My Friend

I had a good friend called Izzy
Who was extremely busy
She worked every day
Until lunchtime - hooray!
But at night-time she felt really dizzy!

Rosie-Mae Shenton (8)
St Thomas Aquinas RC Primary School, Stoke-on-Trent

The Circle Of Life

(Dedicated to Ellen Bamford)

The circle of life is a puzzling thing,
It sometimes can hurt, it sometimes can sting.
When a special someone is there, then not,
I know it can hurt, it can hurt a lot.

But somewhere up there is life beyond the sky,
So please, my dear, don't cry, don't cry.
For even though we are far, far apart,
We're closer than ever, deep in the heart!

Charlotte Barber (11)
St Thomas Aquinas RC Primary School, Stoke-on-Trent

Donkey In A Dream!

One night I dreamt I was riding a donkey
With curly ginger hair on his head
And when I opened my eyes in the morning
The donkey was there in my bed.

I rode into school on my donkey
It caused all the children to scream
But then I did get embarrassed
Guess what? It was just a dream!

I woke up again in my bedroom
Only to realise it was not real
I don't have a ginger-headed donkey
But looking forward to another dream . . .

Baron Ambas (8)
St Thomas Aquinas RC Primary School, Stoke-on-Trent

Kittens In Mittens

K ittens wearing mittens
I magine how cute that would be,
T iny fluffy kittens
T hey are loved by you and me,
E ach one has its own little purr and soft lovely fur,
N oses are as pink as a rose
S oftly miaowing as they pose.

Ryan Holdcroft (8)
St Thomas Aquinas RC Primary School, Stoke-on-Trent

Summer Is Great

Summer is the best season that I have ever known,
In summer no one has got chance to moan,
There are so many things to do,
You can have a big BBQ,
Summer is so cool,
Because you can swim in the swimming pool.

Shannon Holdcroft (9)
St Thomas Aquinas RC Primary School, Stoke-on-Trent

My Best Friend

M illie is my best friend
I always like to help her out
L ovely friends, we like to be kind to each other. If I'm
L onely, she makes me smile
I f I'm sad, she cheers me up
E ven if we have an argument, we're friends again
S ometimes she comes over to my house.

B est friends forever we'll be
E verything is good if I'm with her
S he buys me the best presents in the world
T imes when I'm happy, she makes it better
Millie's best!

Millie Teague (9)
St Thomas Aquinas RC Primary School, Stoke-on-Trent

Springtime!

Spring is here, hip hip hooray
New plants growing, new flowers showing
Beautiful colours everywhere, yellows, orange, pink and white
Oh the colours, what a pretty sight.

Newborn lambs in the meadows skip, bunnies in the underground,
The refreshing smell of the new cut grass
The buds on the trees begin to grow, the seeds in the fields,
                                                farmers sow
Butterflies softly fluttering by, as they gently land on the flowers nearby
Easter eggs and Easter chicks
New life beginning everywhere, yes spring is definitely in the air.

Mollie Cairns (9)
St Thomas Aquinas RC Primary School, Stoke-on-Trent

My England Football Dream

Dear England Team and Manager,

My name is Nyle
And you make me so proud,
I love to be in the football crowd,
You'd know me, I shout very loud.

My name is Nyle,
I dream of playing like you,
Wearing those colours, the red, white and blue,
So I'll watch and I'll copy and pick up some tricks
And I'll learn a dance, for when I score my hat-tricks,

So maybe in a few years time
When the World Cup comes round again
People will wonder where did I hear that name
And I'll say it was *me,* I shout very loud, but now
I'm not just in the crowd.

I love you England!

Nyle Thomas Broadhurst (7)
St Thomas Aquinas RC Primary School, Stoke-on-Trent

Friends Are Forever

F riends are always there for each other
R emembering to care for one another
I think friends are for making you cheer up when you're unhappy,
E verybody cares for their friends.
N o one hates their best friends.
D on't ever lose your friends.

Emily Kendrick (8)
St Thomas Aquinas RC Primary School, Stoke-on-Trent

Camping

Camping is good
Camping is great
Camping is where
You hang out with your mates.

You can go in a caravan
Or in a tent,
You can tell all your friends,
Where you went.

You can like it if
You're 4, 5 or 7.
Even at the age
Of 16 or 11.

In the wide open space,
You can run around,
You can be really loud,
Or not make a sound.

Camping out,
Under the stars,
You might even see
Jupiter or Mars.

Cycling around,
Having lots of fun
Camping is definitely
Number 1!

Sophie Humphrey (9)
Western Primary School, Harrogate

My Dancing Pencil

My dancing pencil
I love my dancing pencil
Not baking, not eating a cake
Not riding a bike or doing revision
My dancing pencil is just twenty times better.

It's tall and thin, moves everywhere
A dancing piece of wood,
It loves to write letters and stories
Does drawings and sketches
But keep it sharp and always to hand.

Luke Kay (9)
Western Primary School, Harrogate

My Guinea Pigs

Warm and snuggly,
Cute and cuddly,
I love you
My guinea pigs!

You sit in your hutch
All quiet and calm,
I want to hold you,
In my palm.

In the night
You sleep in your bed.
In the sun
You have a fluffy head.

In the daytime
You play in your run,
When I look at you,
You have lots of fun.

Bridget Phillip (7)
Western Primary School, Harrogate

Puppy Poem

Five amazing puppies jumping and racing around the garden,
Ruff, ruff, ruff!
Four super pups running round the apple tree,
Ruff, ruff, ruff!!
Three little puppies pulling on a dog lead,
Ruff, ruff, ruff!
Two tiny puppies digging a hole
Ruff, ruff, ruff!
One puppy snuggling into bed
Shhh!

Isabel Peakman (7)
Western Primary School, Harrogate

I Like . . .

I like butterflies
I like bees
I like foxes
I like trees

I like dragonflies
I like snails
I like horses
I like whales

All these things
Are so much fun
Like loving my brother
My dad, my mum!

Jessica Clark (6)
Western Primary School, Harrogate

It Was So Quiet . . .

It was so quiet that I heard
The sun sizzling in the sky.
It was so quiet that I heard
A red rose open.
It was so quiet that I heard
A bee slurping nectar from a flower.
It was so quiet that I heard
The clouds zooming overhead.
It was so quiet that I heard
A snail slithering up the wall.
It was so quiet that I heard
A ladybird flapping his wings.
It was so quiet that I heard
A rainbow spreading across the sky.
It was so quiet that I heard
The stars tinkling in the darkness.
It was so quiet that I heard
My brain thinking.

Poppy Collins (9)
Western Primary School, Harrogate

Violins

Violins are fun to play,
They make me feel so happy.
I can play the violin so come and see today,
I rosin my bow
And stand up tall
And play a little tune I know.
I pull my bow across the strings
And it makes a beautiful sound.
My little sister is very cute when she dances
Round and round.
When I grow up, I wonder where I'll play,
Perhaps I'll play on the stage or even on TV!

Phoebe Hain (6)
Western Primary School, Harrogate

What Am I Going To Write?

My pen and pencil are ready to go,
but what I am going to write, I don't know!
Should I do a story about a baby being fed
or a kangaroo jumping up and down on a bed?
A tornado striking in a Texan town
or a disaster about a house that fell down?
My pen and pencil are ready to go,
but what I am going to write, I don't know?

My blank page is pestering me now,
I need something that makes the teachers shout, 'Wow.'
Should I write a fake letter to my mum and my dad
saying how the weather here is driving me mad?
Or should I write a letter to the council saying, *our street
needs some tidying up to make it neat?*
My pen and pencil are ready to go,
but what I am going to write, I don't know!

Finally, *eureka!* I mean, look at my page
I feel so much better now I'm out of my cage.
Everything written is completely right
and if the teachers disagree I'll put up a fight.
My pen and pencil are ready to go,
what I'm going to write, *I do know!*

Isabella Phillpotts (10)
Western Primary School, Harrogate

Cats

I like cats,
they like me,
they are cute and cuddly.
Some are fury and some are not,
but they like to purr a lot.

Phoebe Van Zelst (7)
Western Primary School, Harrogate

Girlie Girls

Shopping, secrets, things like that
Oh girlie girls they love to chat.
In sleepovers never a wink of sleep.
Celebrities one day they would love to meet.

Make-up, accessories, things for their hair,
In their room, there's the bed and a pink fluffy chair.
When they're older, their cars have to be pink
And also they think that boys stink.

So girls you see, are more than you think,
They lose a nail down the sink.
But girlie girls don't you see,
We'll put you out of your misery.

Charlotte Sadler (10)
Western Primary School, Harrogate

A Mermaid's Tale

Desperately crying, my heart erupts
My face goes white and pale,
I leave my cave in misery and sorrow,
I drag along my tail.

My gold, glistening hair turns rotten and brown,
I can't understand this feeling;
My light blue eyes turn shady grey,
It's revolting and unappealing.

My dad told me about this day,
He told me when I was young,
He said it would be a dreadful time,
I guess he wasn't wrong.

Anna Reed (10)
Western Primary School, Harrogate

Holly My Dog

Holly was my pup,
She was very, very crazy,
I loved her very much!
My dog was very lovely,
But now she is in the world above.
I loved her so much,
It was the good times with Holly I loved very much!
Holly my dog was great. My dog was great.
Over the long time I had her was the best time of my life.
Living with Holly was amazing,
It felt almost like she could speak.
It was fantastic, it was fun
You wouldn't think it would be possible
But Holly was fun,
She was the best and she was mine!

Lauren Mossman (7)
Western Primary School, Harrogate

The Way They Look At Me

It's strange the way they look at me
I don't know why they stare
Is it my clothes, my shoes, my hair?
My friends say they're just jealous
But that I don't believe
There must be a logical reason
Or do they just deceive?
I can't see anything wrong with me
It might be something right
The same thought runs around my mind
When I'm asleep at night
We tried to ask them what it is
But they don't speak a word
It's strange the way they look at me
But that's just what I've heard.

Isobel Woodthorpe (10)
Western Primary School, Harrogate

Wind

Wind, wind go away.
Wind, wind, why do you blow people away?
Wind, we don't need you so please go away!
Wind, wind, why are you so mean?
Is it because you can't be seen?
Wind, wind, what jobs are you useful for?
Please answer before you leave!

Anabel Sampson (8)
Western Primary School, Harrogate

Animals In The Garden

One frog on a lily pad
Two parrots sitting on a tree
Three rabbits go into a little rabbit hole
And the rest go, 'He he he.'

Four snakes slithering in the grass
Five worms keeping very low
Six ladybirds flying by
And the rest go, 'Ho ho ho.'

Seven blind bats hanging upside down
Eight stick insects sitting in a jar
Nine moles digging holes
And the rest go, 'Ha ha ha.'

Henry Boyle (7)
Western Primary School, Harrogate

Miss Muffet - The Real Story

I suppose you've heard about Miss Muffet,
You know, the one who sat on a tuffet.
Not all of that is strictly true,
And I wasn't the one who really said, *boo!*
I was taking a stroll out in the park
'Twas the middle of the night and all was dark.
When suddenly I caught a whiff,
Of curds and whey (so nice to sniff).
I followed it around the place,
And found a girl all dressed in lace.
I asked her then ever so politely,
'Could I have some curds you're clasping so tightly?'
All she did was scream and run,
Didn't even offer me one of her buns!
Her scream was so loud I nearly went deaf,
But I licked up the curds (compliments to the chef)
So now you've heard the real story,
The true one that's much less boring!

Rosie Hilton (10)
Western Primary School, Harrogate

Young Writers Information

We hope you have enjoyed reading this book - and that you will continue to enjoy it in the coming years.

If you like reading and writing poetry drop us a line, or give us a call, and we'll send you a free information pack.

Alternatively if you would like to order further copies of this book or any of our other titles, then please give us a call or log onto our website at www.youngwriters.co.uk

Young Writers Information
Remus House
Coltsfoot Drive
Peterborough
PE2 9JX

(01733) 890066